Common Sense about Fund Raising

by

Robert Keith Leavitt

1949

New York, New York

PRINTED IN THE UNITED STATES BY
AMERICAN BOOK—STRATFORD PRESS, INC., NEW YORK

A FOREWORD

*Concerning the origins and
the factual foundations of
this book*

Among the unquestioned prerogatives of every free-born citizen of this Republic is the privilege of mounting a soap-box and proclaiming that he Speaks for the Public. Any man in good voice can draw a crowd, and thus persuade himself that he heads a Movement. Let him repeat the operation across a state line and it is a National Movement. And next thing you know he is assuring everyone from Kiwanis to Congress that the American Public demands Capital Punishment for Vivisectionists, or Forty Dollars a Week Free to Everyone Over Forty, or a Return to the Old-Time Not-So-Lively Baseball. And the more plausible his Idea—the larger the crowds he can attract—the easier it is for him to convince himself that the American Public, to a man, must be behind him. And since such matters are rarely put to popular vote, there is infrequently any statistical evidence that he is talking through his hat.

This was the case until last summer with the claims put forward in behalf of federated Fund Raising for charity, health and welfare work. Common sense, of course, convinced most people that the idea, for all its attractiveness, was impracticable, and that as such it could scarcely acquire a backing that might be called "demand." But the claims of Federated Fund advocates to a "Mandate from the People" and to "Grass Roots Support" were loud, insistent and in the end disturbing to sincere volunteer workers for causes which the Federated Fund movement would hamstring if not kill. Specifically, people active in the state or local organizations of such bodies as the National Society for Crippled Children and Adults, the American Cancer Society and the National Foundation for Infantile Paralysis wrote to their national headquarters asking, "What bases, if any, have the Federated Fund boosters for claiming Popular Demand?"

There is, in these days, a reliable way to answer any question about what the public is doing or saying: the consumer survey. When a manufacturer wants to be sure whether or not there is a market for a new product, he does not go on anyone's guess or say-so; he engages trained investigators to find out by *asking* people directly and in person. Specifically, he engages a skilled market-research organization to survey an accurately-selected cross-section of the public. That is, a cross-section with accurate proportions of people in all income groups, in all geographic sections of the country, and in cities, towns and farm areas. Such organizations send trained interviewers to ask people directly for their opinions or information *as of the moment.*

This is an important distinction, for it marks the difference between a factual consumer survey and a poll. The former aims strictly to find out and report statistically the facts as they exist during the taking of the survey. The latter aims (or did aim, until a certain recent November) to give *predictive* figures, based on an interpretation of what people said they *would* do.

Factual surveys form the dependable basis of nearly all big-industry operations insofar as they must be shaped to fit public preference. Billions of dollars worth of merchandise, from motor cars to bobby-pins, are designed and made and sold in accordance with the findings of consumer surveys—and safely so, as billions of dollars worth of sales prove every year. To American business, market research in the form of consumer surveys is known as a reliable working tool.

So the National Foundation for Infantile Paralysis did the business-like thing, and engaged a reputable and experienced organization in the field of consumer research to find out what people really thought about the admittedly attractive idea of a Super Fund with just one drive a year. The organization, Charles

C. Flarida, Jr., Inc., of New York, was instructed to find out not only what "the public" thought of the Federated Fund Raising idea, but what was the judgment of representative leaders in business, in organized labor and in health and welfare work itself.

The Flarida organization's interviewers and investigators are located in various representative sections of the country. Not only are these correspondents people of established competence and integrity, but in accordance with sound research practice, they worked without knowing who desired the information, or for what purpose. They had no idea, in other words, whether the data they were after was desired by people in favor of Federated Fund Raising or opposed to it. Their instructions were so carefully drawn to avoid biasing them in favor of independent fund-raising as opposed to the federated method, that in the few cases where people being interviewed said they thought the interviewer was prejudiced, they thought the prejudice was *in favor of Federated Fund Raising*.

The Flarida research included:

—54 interviews with "big business" executives representing 52 firms in all sections of the country.
—49 interviews with executives of fundraising, health, welfare or charitable organizations. Of these, 20 were in organizations presumably favoring feder-

ated fund raising, 29 in agencies believed to be opposed to that idea.

—32 interviews with labor leaders representing both major national groupings and independent labor unions.

—1,006 interviews with ordinary, everyday people in the State of Michigan, where federated fund raising has lately been given considerable publicity. These interviews were distributed in income groups and population-size communities as nearly as possible in proportion to known distribution of the public of that state at large.

—3,992 interviews with ordinary people in the country at large, with similar care taken to obtain a fair cross-section of all income groups, all sizes of city and town, all sections of the country.

Necessarily, many of these interviews, particularly in the groups first mentioned, were subject to the stipulation that respondents would not be directly quoted by name or connection in published findings of the research. The reports of all interviews are, however, preserved for the record in the files of the Flarida organization, whose affidavit appears below.

When the Flarida organization's report was completed and turned in to the Infantile Paralysis people, they found not only that it proved very interestingly what you or any other sensible person might expect—that people at large did *not* favor Federated Fund Raising and that in fact, most of them had never heard of it—but that in the judgments given by business men, labor leaders and fund-raisers there were a great many significant points which should be reported to the Foundation's workers and supporters for their information in discussing a proposal which would affect so adversely the organization in which they were interested and all others of similar character—the so-called national independent agencies: the American Red Cross, the American Cancer Society, the National Tuberculosis Association, the National Society for Crippled Children and Adults and the National Foundation for Infantile Paralysis.

That was where I was called into the picture. In my business as a consultant and writer on public relations, employee relations and the like, I am frequently called upon to analyze statistical findings and to organize them into form for reading. I was engaged, first, to interpret the Flarida report, together with certain other side-light data, for the staff, the volunteer workers and the members of the National Foundation for Infantile Paralysis. In this, I was given a free hand; I could "call 'em as I saw 'em." The National Foundation simply sent me the data without comment or stipulation, and with only the broadest of instructions: to interpret the factual data, such as it was, for the information of their own people. In fact, I never met anyone from the National Foundation in person until my job of writing, in its first stage, was completed.

But in writing what started out as a sheer analysis, I soon found myself writing a plea. The case for independent fund-raising (as at present) against the proposed Super Fund amalgamation for painless giving seemed to me that of a sound, sensible cause as opposed to an attractive, plausible fallacy. In such a situation, the sound cause, because it lacked flashiness, needed temperate, reasonable presentation. And the fallacy, in proportion as it was dazzling, needed analysis into its less gaudy elements for detailed consideration in the light of common sense.

For this purpose I gathered and added to the Flarida data a good deal of published literature from organizations on both sides of the Super Fund question, and drew as well upon much published business experience available in the business press or supplied by national manufacturers or their advertising agencies.

This book seeks to summarize in readable form the case against compulsory federation—i.e. regimentation—in fund-raising on a national scale.

I should like to make clear that this is not an argument against voluntary federation by any agencies which choose to federate for their own reasons and not for the regimentation of others.

Nor is this in any sense an attack on the principle of *local* federation in fund-raising. As the body of the text emphasizes, the local Community Chest is an institution worthy of the highest praise and of all support in its proper field. Independent fund-raising has no case against the Community Chest *as such*, but only against the would-be regimentation of all welfare activities that operate under cover of the Community Chest idea and in some instances from within the shelter of the Community Chest organization itself.

ROBERT KEITH LEAVITT

STATE OF NEW YORK } *ss*
COUNTY OF NEW YORK }

On this 23rd day of Nov., 1948, personally appeared before me Mr. Charles C. Flarida, Jr., President of Charles C. Flarida, Jr., Inc., a corporation having its principal place of business at 420 Lexington Avenue, New York, N. Y., and made oath to the following statement:

The research from which a few statistical findings and many expressions of attitude have been quoted in this book was made by this organization for the National Foundation for Infantile Paralysis, during the summer of 1948. We were commissioned to find facts, not to prove a case, and the Foundation's only stipulation was that procedures must be so thorough and soundly in accord with statistical practice that the facts—whatever they might show—would be unquestionable. We conducted the survey, therefore, exactly as we would any comparable research for a manufacturer: among a cross-section of people carefully chosen for accurate proportion as to geographic, age-and-sex, size-of-community and other factors (including automobile ownership as an indicator of income-distribution), in comparison with latest figures for the country at large. Ample statistical evidence of the accuracy of the cross-section is a part of our records. Similarly, the survey was taken with care to avoid bias in favor of independent fund raising. No interviewer, tabulator or analyst working on the investigation knew until it was finished who the sponsor had been or in which direction, if any, the sponsor's special interest lay. So far as soundness of statistical practice can insure it, we know that this survey presents an accurate picture of the facts within its scope. All the original interviews, together with the tabulations drawn from them, are preserved intact in this office.

(Signed) Charles C. Flarida, Jr.

Subscribed and sworn to before me on this 23rd day of Nov., 1948.

(SEAL)

(Signed) Carolyn E. Jones
Notary Public, State of New York
Residing in New York County
New York Co. Clk's No. 99, Reg. No. 159-J-9
Commission Expires March 30, 1949

"Who can sever love from charity?" asked Shakespeare, voicing in those nine clear syllables the essence of all giving. Without the warmth of generosity, the loving kindness of man to man, there is no giving, but only a parting with money—cold comfort to the weak, barren and tasteless to the strong. "Remember," said St. Paul, "the words of the Lord Jesus, how He said, 'It is more blessed to give than to receive.'" And there is not a man or woman or child who ever truly gave but has felt that blessing in his heart. So if we crush the love out of giving we rob not merely the needy, but the fortunate, whose true fortune consists not in being able to give, but in giving.

Common Sense
about
Fund Raising

IF YOU ARE A CIVIC-MINDED CITIZEN WHO TAKES part in drives to raise money for charity, health, welfare or endowments—or if you are one of those who in every community can be counted on to help worthwhile causes by giving—you are likely to hear a lot of talk sooner or later about a Wonderful New Idea in fund-raising—a sort of Community Chest on a national scale, with everybody in it and just one drive a year. The idea goes by various names: Federated Fund Raising; a National Chest; the Super Chest; the Single Fund; United Fund Raising; the Single Federated Fund Raising Campaign . . . It has various extra features, and people have different ideas for working it out, but essentially it is a Super Community Fund. You should know about that idea, both so that you can judge it for yourself, and so that you can discuss it intelligently with others.

For the Super Chest idea is so attractive that many people take it up without stopping to reflect whether or not it would work. Here—paraphrased for conciseness—is the case as its proponents state it. Their reasoning is so plausible that anyone may be forgiven for not immediately perceiving the flaws in it:

"Giving in America has become so extensive that there are more fund-raising drives than people know what to do with. The average man or woman or organization is bothered to distraction with them. Givers are confused among many causes, about most of which they have little direct information. Some of these causes seem to duplicate one another, and they all compete for the same amount of dollars the public has to give.

"The way to solve this difficulty would be to get all the worthy causes and agencies together in one big drive. That is, have a Super Community Chest that would include everything: Red Cross, Tuberculosis, Cancer, March of Dimes—and all the other big nation-wide agencies—as well as the local ones already included in the Community Chest . . . and any deserving new ones that come along. Then the giver would not be bothered except once a year; volunteer workers would have to work only once a year; and all the money could be collected at once—at a great deal less cost for collection.

"There would be another advantage in this: the total amount of money could be portioned out very fairly among agencies according to their need or their deserts, as judged by the Super Chest authorities, instead of being competed for, the way it is now.

"This power to control funds would in time make it possible for the Super Chest authorities to oversee the operations of all agencies and make sure they conducted themselves efficiently. For instance, the Super Chest people could make them stop duplicating or competing with one another. It they failed to cooperate in such matters they could be starved out of existence. In fact, there are probably some charities right now that ought to be killed off.

"The first step toward this is to set up in each locality a sort of screening committee or appeals review board or authority to review all proposed city-wide or state-wide or nation-wide fund-raising campaigns and say (1) whether they are

3

approved; (2) if so, how much they might seek in the community. This would protect givers, for they could refuse to give to drives that were not approved. So organizations that could not secure approval would soon learn to stay away. And others —even the most popular—would not take more out of the community than the amount the committee decided was their proper share. It would also pave the way for eventually forcing all organizations to come in on a Super Chest as soon as one could be organized.

"This idea, in its essence, has the approval of most professional Community Chest executives. It is favored by experts, including several who have recommended it in books. It is also favored by civic bodies and many very prominent business men. In fact, in communities where it has been proposed, it is favored by large numbers of thinking people."

That last paragraph is very true. The people who originally conceived this plan are men and women of the highest sincerity, animated by ideals above reproach. The people who support it include citizens of the most unquestioned integrity; people whose life work is bound up with health, welfare or fund-raising; business and professional men of international repute. The people in any community who favor the Super Fund idea are responsible people of the thinking type.

Yet it must be said that large numbers of people of equally high standing believe the Super Fund idea is a mistake—an attractive one, but founded on the hasty overlooking of certain common-sense facts. Among those who have expressed opposition to the Super Fund idea are not only many men and women prominent as individuals, but most of the leading national organizations in health and welfare work— the so-called national independent agencies. These include the American National Red Cross, the American Cancer Society, the National Foundation for Infantile Paralysis, the National Society for Crippled Children and Adults, the National Tuberculosis Society and others known in every household for their long and devoted service to the cause of health and welfare in America.

When people and organizations of such standing question the advisability of a proposal, it is worth while to examine the reasons for their doubts.

The Basic Fallacy

Basically, the trouble with the Super Fund idea is that it is founded on wishful thinking. Fascinated with the immediately-attractive hope of getting all giving taken care of with a minimum of bother to the giver, its converts convince themselves that the common sense which shapes and guides our everyday activities will somehow turn out not to apply to fund-raising. They know that common sense has to govern our conduct of business, science, education, government . . . even the exercise of religious freedom. But the happy vision of being asked to give only once a year blinds them to the fact that both giving and asking are subject to common sense.

Specifically, there are laws of human nature and principles of economics and fundamental considerations of liberty that govern fund-raising and administration, just as they do all other activities of life. You cannot regiment business or science, education or religion into Utopian patterns without devitalizing them—you have only to look at totalitarian regimes to see that. Yet business men whose whole success is founded upon typical American initiative, enterprise and freedom of action became so fascinated with the bright picture of not being "pestered" that they fall for a novel proposal without realizing that it would regiment charity and welfare straight along totalitarian lines.

In all fairness to these people, it should be said that the facts they overlook are very easy ones to miss—for two reasons, each applying to a different kind of facts: One class of facts is so simple and familiar and everyday that it is easy for us to forget their very existence—like amateurs planning a house and forgetting to allow space for the stairs. The other class of facts consists of specialized information not all of us have. Some of these facts relate to the laws of human nature in mass reaction; some of them relate to the economics of business; some of them relate to specific practices in fund raising . . .

It is facts of this sort which, if you consider them fairly, will show you the first big difficulty with the Super Fund plan:

A Super Fund Could Not Collect Sufficient Money

There is a very plausible statement usually made by people who talk up the Super Fund idea: "A single fund each year would bring in as much or more money than the sum of all drives that could be put on by its members." This is plausible because on a small scale, as in the case of Community Chests in their drives for local agencies, it is usually true. It is misleading because on a large scale, as applied to year-round welfare efforts and large national health and welfare agencies, it would work in reverse: the total amount of money obtained would be far less than at present.

A single effort works out well for the usual Community Chest for one reason: Most of the local member agencies of the usual Chest are not strong enough in workers and resources, or skilled enough in fund-raising, to get the best results by themselves. And some of them are agencies with inadequate popularity, as in the case of colored agencies in some southern cities. By uniting forces, local agencies get the benefits of a large organization, skilled direction, plenty of enthusiastic workers, adequate publicity, nation-wide timing and a strong popular appeal. The city or county Community Chest is a great thing for American local welfare work.

But because a thing is successful on a small scale does not necessarily mean that it would be successful on a large one. That would be like saying, "Students can live most successfully in dormitories; therefore families of adults should live in dormitories."

And there is another thing about the Community Chest. The reason it is a great institution is not because it lessens "bother" for the giver or confines "annoyance" to one brief season. That is a purely incidental effect. The real justification of a local Community Chest is that it is an efficient way to combine *small* fund-raising efforts into one larger one. People do not give more because they are bothered *less*, but because they are bothered *more efficiently*.

Yet people given to wishful thinking often attribute the success of a local campaign to its freedom from "annoyance." Then they add to that error another one: the "dormitory" kind of reasoning mentioned above. And they come up with something like this:

> "A single drive each year, to include everybody, from the Red Cross down, would bring in as much or more money than all the present ones, because it would be more attractive to industry and to the individual, who would give more freely."

Now that just does not happen to be true. In fact, it is against all business experience and all everyday common sense.

Once a Year Is Not Enough

Every industrial concern knows this. Not one company in a thousand would try to sell its annual output in a single, brief campaign. In fact, the very executive whose statement is used almost word-for-word above is employed by an automobile firm famous for its unremitting pressure, its continuous advertising and its intensive seasonal drives for business. Doubtless in his sincere enthusiasm for a novel idea, he had forgotten that the raising of funds totalling many millions of dollars is also a matter for businesslike planning.

A newspaper publisher who, in the flush of a public

appearance, made substantially similar statements, had apparently forgotten that his paper comes out not once a year, but every day in the year, and that it lives on the advertising of department stores smart enough to realize the necessity of recurring sales, and of manufacturers who know that if you are going to coax people to give you their dollars, you have got to keep everlastingly at it.

When individuals in such positions make a claim contrary to the experience and policy of their own organizations, it is evident that they do so hastily and without considering all the facts.

On the other hand, many executives representing corporations of equal prominence, give it as their sound judgment that a single fund-raising campaign could not possibly hope to equal in effectiveness the present system of several drives by voluntary independent organizations, spread out over a year. Though several of these big business representatives are frank to say that it would save trouble for themselves and their corporations to handle all donations in one decision, they add with emphasis that such a plan would be impractical for many reasons, and especially that it would not raise adequate funds for the needs of charity and welfare.

This is because they have taken into consideration (as the wishful thinkers have not) a basic law of human behavior known to all American business concerns, from the largest to the smallest. It can be expressed in concrete terms:

The average man or woman would rather part with $5 every month or two than spend $20 right now.*

The ordinary citizen will part with only just so much money at any given time. The amount he will give depends upon his circumstances, but it is normally on the cautious side. He will disburse not what reason tells him he could afford out of a year's budget, but what caution lets him unbelt between now and next pay-day.

Yet this same ordinary citizen will spend, month by month, as he sees his way clear, a far greater sum—clear up to the margin of his income.

It is this fact which keeps in existence the stores, the wholesalers, the manufacturers . . . in fact, all commerce and industry in this country.

Economic law is no mystery, and it cannot be changed by wishful thinking. Just as every gardener

---

* Even the Super Fund advocates recognize this. Not long ago a group of them were asked, "Do you believe the average man would rather give $5 six times a year or $20 right now?" 88% said, "$5 six times a year." As a check on this, first a group of labor leaders and then 3,992 ordinary citizens were asked the same question. Their answers show that in this respect not even wishful thinking can blind the Super Fund people to the facts of human nature:

	Super Fund Advocates	Labor Leaders	Ordinary Citizens
People would rather give $5 six times a year	88%	83%	77%
People would rather give $20 right now	12%	0%	19%
Don't know, or no opinion	0%	17%	4%

knows that you can get more roses by cutting them daily than by gathering them once a season, so every business man knows that *you can get more money from people by year-round effort than you ever would by once-a-year appeals.*

Fund-raising may not be selling (though many businessmen volunteers and professional workers find that it makes sense to speak of it as such), but it is at least subject to the same laws of human nature. For this reason, a single drive—no matter what pressure was massed behind it—could not possibly begin to gather as much for charity, health and welfare work as is now gathered by the year-round efforts of Community Chests, Red Cross Roll Call, Tuberculosis Stamps, The March of Dimes, and so on.

Many (but not all) of the Super Fund supporters themselves realize that this is true. Typical of those who face facts thus frankly is one who says, "People who can't afford to make their annual charitable contributions at one time manage better with multiple drives, to which they give on a sort of installment plan." Then the same Fund executive deals just as frankly with his own colleagues' belief that installment giving—by monthly pledges—would get around human reluctance to give the maximum at any one time. "The average man," he says, "probably could cover himself by pledges, but he doesn't like to feel indebted."

Installment Pledges Are Not the Answer

While it is true that many Americans habitually *buy* on the installment plan, it is not true that they habitually *give* in that fashion. The plain fact is that people let themselves in for time payments only with reluctance and only when they can pay in no other way. Many people will not buy on installment at all (74% of car purchases are paid in cash, 58% of electrical appliances, 41% of furniture). And every volunteer fund-raiser knows that large numbers of people give less than they could afford, rather than pledge themselves to time payments.

Harold J. Seymour, former General Manager of the National War Fund, adds in his book *Design for Giving*, "Chest experience has long since indicated that anyone is likely to give more on the installment plan . . . than in one cash gift, but that pledges . . . [are] difficult to collect unless . . . by authorized payroll deductions . . . the 'check-off.' "

Human Nature in One-Time Giving

There is another quirk in human nature, too, which operates to cut down on funds raised in a single-drive campaign. It is known to every experienced worker in fund-raising: Many people give less in total when they can appease their consciences by giving only once a year. As one New York welfare worker puts it, they "hide behind their contributions to the Greater New York Fund because it is easier and they can give much less." And workers in another Atlantic Coast city tell with grim amusement of "a large giver [who] used to give $100,000 a year to a number of charities. When the Chest took over, he reduced his contribution to $50,000, and everybody thought it was wonderful." In Detroit, the center of Super Fund propaganda, supporters of that very idea acknowledge ruefully a "tendency of the individual to give less when he gives as part of an organization."

The next reason why a Super Fund would fail to raise adequate funds is also based on a set of human-nature facts which the advocates of federated fund-raising fail to take into account:

A Super Fund Would Be Weakened by Diffusion of its "Appeal"

A few thoroughgoing Utopians among Super Fund advocates are fond of saying that money should ideally be raised without any emotional appeal at all, but simply by telling people that such-and-such an amount was needed. Most advocates of the single fund would not go so far. But many of them are almost as unworldly in their naive misunderstanding of what you need for a successful appeal. One widely-quoted book by a pair of earnest Utopians puts it this way:

> "If effectively presented to the public, the idea of health promotion and disease prevention in such concrete terms as prevention of blindness, conservation of hearing, healthy childbirth, prevention of mental breakdown, sane education for family responsibilities, elimination of syphilis or gonorrhea, safeguarding one's heart and increasing the usefulness of the public health nurse, would make a profounder impression than the present hit-or-miss contact with just one appeal . . ." *

Now, these idealists' theory of how to make an effective appeal is completely at variance with the practical experience of all businessmen. Indeed, every merchant or manufacturer who advertises or makes a drive to sell merchandise knows that if you want to succeed, you have to emphasize *one principal selling point at a time*, and that if you try to

---

* Gunn and Platt, *Voluntary Health Agencies*, New York, The Ronald Press Co., 1945, pp. 223-4. Of this book Dr. D. B. Armstrong, former President of the National Health Council, said in the *Journal* of the American Medical Association for June 15, 1946, that it was "the work of a self-created committee . . . [which took] five years of scurrying around the country [and] $100,000 [to produce] obvious suggestions . . . which could . . . have been outlined in a few hours by anyone familiar with the field."

tell people all the good things about your product at once and with equal emphasis, you simply weaken your appeal by diffusion.

If, for example, you are making and selling an automobile, you may choose at any given time to emphasize "NEW" as Ford did when it brought out 1948 models. Doubtless Ford could also have emphasized beauty, durability, economy, safety, comfort, driving ease, service and many other features. But to have done so would have weakened that season's appeal by dilution. Follow the advertising of other manufacturers—and of retailers, too—and you will see how carefully this principle is followed by men whose business it is to know human nature. For people react to sharply-defined and specific appeals, not to diffused, sprawling collections of every argument anyone can think up.

Men who know welfare work, business and human nature say the same thing about fund-raising. An official of one of America's largest life insurance companies says, "The grouped method [of fund-raising] would kill off support by generalizing the appeal. Most people give to particular charities because they have a special interest in the work conducted by those charities." A labor leader who would be inclined to favor a single fund if it would work, says it is unlikely to work because "it is necessary to educate the public first . . . Tell the public what the drive is for . . . Emotional appeal is needed . . . Here the independents are . . . able to cite strong

and convincing reasons that draw out contributions
... They reach a greater diversity of prospects and
their appeals are ... identified with a definite cause."
And even professional fund-raisers sympathetic to
the Super fund movement concede that "independents, with their emotional and dramatic appeals, get
the most money."

A striking example of the way in which a drive
can fail when its appeal is weakened by diffusion
occurred as recently as spring, 1948. A group of 26
hitherto-independent agencies for aid to children in
various countries overseas were persuaded to federate
in one drive, the American Overseas Aid merged with
the United National Appeal for Children. Despite
enormous press and radio publicity, including powerful support given by General Eisenhower and
others, the drive failed dismally to produce adequate
funds.

Another set of human-nature facts is similar to
those just cited in reducing the effectiveness of a
Super Fund:

A Super Fund Would Suffer Through Loss of Personal Interest by Givers and Workers

Every experienced fund-raiser knows that people
give most generously to causes in which they have a
lively personal interest, through natural inclina-

tion, sentiment, personal experience, membership-affiliation or participation in work. And it is common experience that the more agencies are grouped in a federated fund (such as a Community Chest), the harder it is to arouse this personal interest.

In fact, Mr. Lynn D. Mowat, General Manager of the Welfare Fund of Los Angeles, in an article pleading the cause of federated fund-raising, says, "Some chests have forgotten that they are federations of *givers' interests* as well as of agencies, and have too often excluded causes in which givers were definitely interested . . . People want to give to combat things they dislike and dread . . . cancer, heart disease, venereal disease, infantile paralysis, mental disease . . ." And numerous respondents to the survey cited in the front of this book mentioned other special interests. Exclude a giver's favorite charity and he or she is apathetic to a fund's appeal. And even when his favorite is included, his interest in it is diluted by the inclusion of other agencies for which he has no special enthusiasm.

Much more pronounced is the effect of federation upon workers. The keenest volunteers are those with the most powerful personal interest in a specific cause. As Seymour says of the Red Cross success, "Loyalty is born of interest, and interest is the child of participation." A Y.M.C.A. official puts it much the same way: "Independent fund-raising gives more opportunity for self-expression of people as leaders and workers. In a group effort this would be lost."

And Chest officials themselves add, "The Chest can induce mental laziness," and, "The Councils and Chests . . . [are] losing or have not sufficiently encouraged the active participation of citizens at large." It is inevitable that a Super Fund's all-inclusiveness would fail to enlist the special interest of many exceedingly valuable workers.

All-inclusiveness has, in fact, a negative influence upon some givers. As every Chest worker has learned, there are many people who will not give a nickel to a Chest if it includes an agency they dislike or distrust. Big-business men and other givers of substantial sums are emphatic on this point.

Now it is trustingly believed by many advocates of the Super Fund idea that it would be possible to overcome the various objections quoted in the last few pages, by allowing donors to designate how their gifts should be distributed. This practice, they say, is common in Community Chest work, and makes it possible for the giver with special interests to make sure that his money reaches his favorite agencies and no others. But actually this is a sheer delusion.

Designation by Givers is Discouraged or Even Cynically Disregarded by Typical Chests

"If grouped activity does not respect the individual's request regarding allocation of funds, the activity will lose many donations," says the General

Director of a highly regarded Foundation, who personally favors federated fund-raising. He is correct, but apparently unaware that many professional Chest people, the would-be operators of a national Super Chest, regard givers' designation as an unmitigated nuisance, expensive and bothersome to handle, insulting to the dignity of Chest authorities and deserving to be discouraged by all practicable means.

Many Chests, even though they hold this view, are scrupulous to see that designations are conscientiously carried out. "Allocations are permitted but not encouraged . . . They are now negligible, [Note: "Negligible" in this case is a doubtful term; some 40% of the money in the respondent's city was designated.] mostly by small crackpot givers. They are indeed respected."

A stiffer note is sounded in another city: "Designation is wrong in principle. Everybody does not have to believe in every agency . . . Altogether, there would be too much confusion and agitation by encouraging designation to individual charities and therefore it is not considered satisfactory." (A business man in this Chest authority's town pointed out that the Chest did not any longer put on its cards a space for designation.)

Or again, in another city, "If people want to designate where their contributions shall go, they may, but . . . the Committee should decide what each agency needs."

This last hints at a practice that appears to be widespread: the giver can designate, and his favorite charity gets notified that he has designated his money for it—*but the charity gets no more money in the end than its set quota.*

In one large city the Executive Director of the Community Fund says, "A giver may designate his pet charity, but this is not printed on the card. Designations are recognized to be binding only up to the budget quota."

In another large city the Director of a screening bureau says, "Designation of particular charities in giving to the Chest means nothing at all. They are a selling device worthy of commercial advertising, but are not respected to any important respect in Chest financing."

Are these isolated cases or common practice? Here is what two well informed fund-raising people say of cities other than their own. Says one, "Fund raisers in general dislike designation. It is generally respected, but has no over-all importance, since the sum of the designated gifts rarely reaches the total budget for any member agency and Chests generally reserve the right to make their own allocation of any designations over the budget quota." And the other continues, "It is the acknowledged Chest policy in most localities that designation will be respected to the aggregate of the [agency's] budgeted share of the drive goal. Any excess is to be allotted as part of the general fund."

In other words, a policy common among Community Chests is to allow the giver to think he is designating for one particular charity, but actually to nullify that gift by allotting a corresponding number of other dollars elsewhere. That this policy would be followed by a Super Chest is almost inevitable: the cost-and-trouble factors would be infinitely greater in such a Chest, and the people who would form its policies are the very people who now shape the techniques of local Chests.

Another internal policy of Chest administrators which is also little known would similarly have an adverse effect upon fund-raising:

Setting Area Limits for National Agencies Prevents Their Reaching a National Quota

One policy already adopted in certain areas where Screening Boards and local Chest authorities seek to control the giving to national organizations is plausible—but extremely unsound:

> "If the 'drive' is a national one . . . [its] local quota must not exceed a 'yardstick' formula adopted as the city's equitable share of the organization's national goal, as based on certain indexes of population,

> earnings, employment, trade, standard-of-
> living factors and the like."

That is, the independent national fund-raising agency (Red Cross, Tuberculosis, Cancer, Salvation Army or whatever it is) must take no more out of any one town than the exact amount corresponding to the proportionate size and wealth of the town in the national economy.

On the face of it, that is plausible. But reflect. Fund-raising is like any other activity that consists of a number of separate parts. In order to reach an *over-all* quota you have to exceed average in some places, because you inevitably fall below it in others. It's like football: if a team is going to gain 10 yards in four downs ($2\frac{1}{2}$ yards per down), it must occasionally gain more than $2\frac{1}{2}$ yards to make up for the times it gets stopped dead at the line of scrimmage. To say to a welfare agency, "You must not take more than 1% of your goal from our city," is like saying to a football team, "You must not gain over $2\frac{1}{2}$ yards on any play." No team, no organization, can achieve an over-all goal without exceeding the average somewhere.

The National War Fund discovered this by hard experience. Says Mr. Seymour, its wartime director, "To expect success in every city, state or community is simply beyond the limits of human experience. Even one failure, therefore, by so much as one dollar in a single town will mean national failure unless there is a margin to balance such loss . . . In any multiple fund-raising effort where there is likelihood that some units will succeed and some will fail, total success can be assured only by adopting . . . one or both of two measures: including in the goal an extra amount as a . . . safety factor against unit failures, or an agreement that successful units will either pay the full amounts raised . . . or will share such over-subscription in some equable proportion." But the Super Fund planners do not appear to realize that this is essential.

No Analogy to National War Fund

People who want very much to believe in the Super Fund idea despite its obvious weaknesses sometimes fall back on the analogy of the National War Fund. "Why!" they exclaim, "the National War Fund was really nothing but a Super Chest! It raised large sums—ample sums—at low cost. A Super Fund in time of peace would do as well."

A little reflection will show why this is not so. Consider the special factors affecting the National War Fund. None of them would apply to a Super Fund in time of peace:

1. Wartime enthusiasm, fervor and devotion on the part of every citizen, far beyond that of peace years.

2. An appeal for service to the Armed Forces and civilian victims of war. This was a sharp and definite appeal, a highly emotional appeal and an appeal in which practically everyone in the country had a personal interest as father, mother, brother, sister, sweetheart, friend, neighbor or employer of someone to be benefited by the War Fund.

3. Cumulative effect of all other war publicity for production, saving, Red Cross, victory gardens, war bonds . . . an endless stream of publicity centered around the idea of self-sacrifice.

4. The feeling of personal debt on the part of those at home who could not serve, toward those who were serving.

5. Many organizations and individuals gave their services on a scale that could not possibly be duplicated in peacetime: labor unions, corporations, clubs, societies, publishers, billboard people, radio networks, motion pictures, speakers, entertainers, advertising experts, artists and unnumbered hosts of volunteer workers. The War Fund got $30,000,000 worth of donated publicity at a cost of less than $1,000,000.

6. In many instances organizations such as companies and unions brought to bear

on their employees or members a pressure for unanimity of contributions which would not be tolerated in peacetime.

7. Incomes were at a high point up to that time; prices were low; employment was universal; there was more money for giving.

8. Over all the nation was a sense of unity and an awareness of the importance of finishing the task of which this was a part.

All these factors combined to produce an effect which everybody but a Utopian recognizes could not possibly be duplicated in time of peace. A significant indication of this is that as soon as peace became certain the National War Fund encountered, according to Mr. Seymour, its wartime director, "both the general letdown and confusion following V-J Day and the difficulty of holding together the state and local machinery for collection." The fund fell short of its 1945 goal by some $28,000,000, or 24%.

A Super Fund Would Not Get Everybody In

For the same reasons that a Super Fund would fail to get as much money as a series of continuing drives, it would fail to get in as many people. To reach everybody, you must have a variety of appeals. Not one appeal of the everything-but-the-kitchen-stove kind, but a number of separate appeals, so that people interested in fighting cancer, say, but not in general health or welfare work could find a place and an interest. Or so that those who feel that the big popular causes are well taken care of could devote themselves to the small, little-known ones.

A Super Fund Would Not Work Economically

The physical overhead of operating a single fund would be enormous, despite the fact that it functioned only once a year. To do the job of investigating, allocating, overseeing and policing all causes—as that job is envisioned by the Super Fund advocates—would require a small army of trained, highly-paid bureaucrats. To raise even half-way-adequate funds by a giant super-drive once a year would require an even greater army of paid fund-raisers and their helpers. This staff would either have to be kept together throughout the year for perhaps five months of work, or would have to be even more expensively recruited and trained for the annual peak effort. To house these twin armies would require an entire office building of considerable size for headquarters; regional headquarters throughout the nation.

Would these armies justify their existence by replacing an equivalent number of workers now employed by the national independent agencies? By no means, for the staffs of the independent agencies are engaged only in small part in the raising of funds. The primary objective and the principal work of health and welfare agencies is in their programs of caring for and lessening the incidence of disease or distress. Fund-raising is purely secondary with them. Even if they never had to take time for it, their organizations would have to be maintained in very large part—as were the operating organizations of the agencies whose funds came in wartime from the National War Fund.

A far more serious matter is the fact that a Super Fund's budget could be raised only at prohibitive cost. For the more money you raise at one time— i.e., the farther you extend your drive to clean up every available cent—the higher will be your operating costs per dollar of funds raised. It is· the old economists' Law of Diminishing Returns.

This "law" is simply an expression of experience common in everyday life: You can raise 3 tons of hay on an acre of land by the use of, say, 500 pounds of a certain kind of fertilizer. But add another 500 pounds and you don't get 3 more tons of hay; you only get about 1 more. Beyond a normal yield, the going gets harder. Or again, anyone who ever pumped up a tire by hand knows that the last ten pounds of pressure take more pumping than the first twenty. In fact, everyone who has had experience in fund-raising comes in contact with the Law of Diminishing Returns. If you set out to compile a list of the people living in a given neighborhood, you can get it 90% quite easily—in an afternoon, say. But to make that list 100% complete and accurate may take a whole additional day or more. If you set out after contributions from the people on a street, you can often find 90% of them at home and get their contributions in one single trip. But to see *all* of them and get pledges from *all* of them may take several additional trips, each as long and troublesome as the first.

It is the same way with drives as a whole. Any one drive at any one time can get a normal amount fairly easily. But exceeding that amount is possible only at a cost that rises prohibitively with every additional increment collected. Seymour, himself an advocate of some form of federated health and welfare work (though not, apparently, of a one-shot drive), says, "The effectiveness of campaign organizations is limited by the Law of Diminishing Returns . . . the wider its periphery, the lower its returns and the greater the proportional cost . . . Most of the cost is involved in raising the last 10% of the money."

For publicity alone, a Super Fund would find itself committed to a sum of money measurable only in multi-millions. Figure it out for yourself. The National War Fund needed $10 million worth of publicity each year (mostly donated, but measurable in dollars nonetheless) to raise $115 million annually. That is less than two-fifths of the $300 million a Super Fund would have to raise if it were to cover even minimum existing requirements of all agencies it would pretend to serve. It raised $115 million at a cost of $10 million in wartime. But in 1945, when the spur of war urgency was withdrawn, $10 million worth of publicity brought in only $87 million—*not thirty per cent* of the amount that would be needed by a Super Fund.

Could you raise $300 million in one drive by spending two and a half or three times $10 million? Certainly not, any more than the farmer can get three times as much hay from one field by piling on three times as much fertilizer. Yet that, seemingly, is the expectation of the Super Fund advocates. The net result would be not merely failure, but failure at a cost of fantastic millions spent in the attempt.

Would the greater part of these millions be donated, as in wartime, in the form of space, radio time, materials and services? It is doubtful. But even if they were, that would still constitute expenditure out of the nation's pocket, for *somebody* has to pay for whatever is donated.

Multiple drives, spaced out over the year, can and do raise $300 million a year, at a cost infinitely less than a single Super Fund drive would incur in vainly attempting to reach that mark.

One Super Fund Would Not Take Care of All Deserving Organizations

When they are talking at large, as for the purpose of interesting busy businessmen, the Super Fund people are fond of implying that one federated fund would take care of all agencies that now solicit money for any praiseworthy purpose and dispose of those which are not worthy. But when they come to discuss the practical details of a proposed Super Fund, they acknowledge that neither of those two ends could possibly be achieved.

To begin with, many agencies are completely outside the scope of any federated fund. All agencies of specialized interest—scientific, research, educational, religious, fraternal, labor and the like—would be excluded from a national Super Fund for reasons of policy. So would all capital and endowment fund-raising moves. This would leave many thousands of worthy causes—national, regional, local or specialized—either without support or under the necessity of campaigning for their own funds in the face of a public sentiment systematically trained to refuse all non-fund solicitations.

Again, it would tend to freeze out, almost at birth, even the most worthy of new organizations. Present Chest policy is to require a local agency to demonstrate its fitness by a year or two of independent fund-raising before it is admitted to the Chest. Under a Super Fund which discouraged the public from giving to anyone *except* the Fund, such agencies would have extreme difficulty even to get started.

And even among agencies admitted to—or forced to join—Chests, it is common experience in Community Chest work that provision for member agencies is all too often inadequate. "New agencies," says a typical Chest executive, "often receive less than they had previously raised," and another Chest director adds, "When an agency enters the fund, sometimes this is a hardship, and sometimes its program is curtailed." The Gunn-Platt report says, "An agency once admitted has a better chance of keeping its status than of getting an increased allotment for urgently needed work." In many cities, agencies, after trying to manage on reduced budgets allotted to them by Chests, have withdrawn and, as independents again, have without difficulty raised annual budgets of three, four or more times the share which the Chest could raise for them. And this without any discernible effect whatever upon the Chest's drives the same years.

A Super Fund Would Not Eliminate "Annoyance"

The convert to Super Fund ideas is usually most powerfully attracted by the idea that under such a happy Utopian regime he would not be subject to today's "annoyances" of multiple solicitations. This is a mirage, as most Chest people know very well. There are scores of eminently worthy causes in every region, whose work or nature makes them ineligible to Chest membership. Let no college alumnus suppose that Alma Mater is not going to brace him two or three times a year. The veterans' associations, the fraternal orders, the unions, the churches with all their missionary societies, and so on down to the innumerable Police Orphans' Funds, Firemen's Hallowe'en Parties, Neighborhood Association Outings and the like—all are outside the scope of an ordinary Chest, to say nothing of a Super Chest. Yet almost without exception they can prove a right to ask for support.

Indeed, the chief advocates of Super-Funding recognize that it would be impossible completely to deny organizations, large and small, the right to raise funds in their own way, even if they were included in the Fund. With an obvious respect for such accepted and beloved drives as the Red Cross Roll Call and the Christmas sale of Tuberculosis Seals, the Gunn-Platt report itself says, "Other sources of income would need to be permitted [to independent agencies], including memberships, sales of literature and supplies . . ."

Any fair count of your own daily mail, any fair tabulation of time demanded of you by visitors or callers-by-phone, will show that only a small part of it originates with agencies which could by any stretch of policy be consolidated in a national Super Fund drive. "There is no 'annoyance' from recognized agencies," says one big-business executive, "just from the little-known organizations." The greater part of the so-called "annoyance" comes from the solicitation of organizations that could not be covered by a Super Fund. Nor could most of them be liquidated, even by pressure of public opinion pumped up by a Super Fund; they have, as more than one Chest executive has ruefully observed, "too strong a local acceptance ever to be done away with."

Are People Really "Annoyed"?

We have been talking about "annoyance" and "bother" as though those were really grave troubles which urgently demand alleviation. But is that really so?

Granted that it is always troubling to the spirit to be reminded that there is distress abroad in the world—sometimes perhaps entering our own homes—and that it is never pleasant to think of parting with money—even for so necessary a matter as today's groceries. But let us admit that disturbing thoughts are an inevitable part of normal existence for anyone who can not withdraw from the realities of life by an ostrich-like burying of his head in the sand or a dreamer's retirement into the world of Utopian fantasy. The rest of us have to face realities, and we know it does not eliminate those realities to close the door of a sickroom or to throw bills into the wastebasket unopened. We would rather face such realities directly than to put them off—as some Super Chest advocates would—upon taxation. We cannot agree with those who would like merely to postpone the "annoyance" of giving money by the proposal: "All charities should be eliminated and the entire matter made a federal burden . . . supported by taxation." So we accept direct calls on our generosity as a matter of duty—and we are not as seriously troubled by those calls as the Super Fund advocates believe.

Why Some—But Not All—Industrialists Find Charity "Annoying"

The Super Fund advocates are fond of quoting some big-business executives as saying that there are too many requests for giving. Now while there are very many big-business men who do *not* feel this way, it is worth considering why even *some* of them do.

When a business leader allows himself to be quoted to this effect, he is usually speaking from one of two standpoints: (1) as the head of a corporation asked to give as such, or to cooperate in getting its employees to give; (2) as an individual forced by his position to allot what he considers an undue amount of time to listening to pleas for funds.

Corporation Convenience

A corporation *as such* may logically prefer federated giving and federated administration of its gifts from corporate funds, as distinct from the organized gifts of its employees or the individual gifts of its executives. That saves a certain amount of executives' and board-of-directors' time; it saves budgeting and bookkeeping trouble; it saves charges of favoritism in giving; and it saves time "lost" when employees devote a part of their efforts to fundraising. If a corporation is—as some contend—obliged to be strictly hard boiled in its attitude toward giving, these are logical considerations. A corporation, too, may often contend with justice that it is not—like the individual—likely to give more in response to several requests than to one, since its total budget for contributions is often set by board-of-directors' action.

These considerations should be borne in mind, even though corporate gifts *as such* form only a minority of the total contributed by giving America to the cause of charity, health and welfare.

The executive *as an individual* is, however, influenced by other considerations.

The Big Executive's Personal "Annoyance"

Many—but by no means all—big executives allow
their view of charity and fund-raising to be colored
by a purely personal reaction to a situation peculiar
to men in their positions. It is perhaps a natural reaction to a curious and interesting circumstance:
listening to appeals for charity is almost the only
detailed activity which the "big shot" cannot dele-
gate. He can appoint administrators to handle all
details of production, engineering, sales, advertising
. . . and people who have business with his firm must
deal with these executives—or else. But when it comes
to charity, the people who approach him are his own
friends and associates, or his wife's or daughter's
friends, or his customers or their friends. These people will not be put off with a "rubber-stamp" front
man; they insist on seeing the "big shot" himself. It
is no wonder that many top industrial executives find
the multiple calls of charity a vastly time-consuming
matter.

The Broader View

Not all big-business men, of course, consider this
a burden unworthy of a leader, or one beyond his
capability to handle. "Annoyance," says an executive
of one of the country's greatest corporations, "is not

a serious factor," and another—also representing one of our biggest companies—says, "Multiple drives may seem annoying to many, until people realize that charitable work is a vital part of the American way of life." Still another top industrial executive, while conceding that grouped fund-raising would be easier for him, adds that he does not find it difficult to deal adequately and fairly with even the present multiple demands. Nor is he deceived into thinking that a grouped activity would consolidate all requests. "Good causes," he says, "can best be developed independently . . . The bigger charities get, the more responsibilities they assume, and the more good they do."

The Ordinary Citizen is Too Sensible to be "Annoyed"

For the average citizen the so-called "annoyance" of multiple solicitation is by no means as great as Super Fund advocates like to represent it. The ordinary householder, even in a highly civic-minded community, is rarely called upon in a whole year to give as much time to all personal solicitations put together as he puts in at one session of mowing his lawn. And if a few people find it an "intolerable annoyance" to receive letters asking for money, most of us are mature enough to decide quickly and without going emotionally to pieces whether an appeal deserves to be referred to the check-book or to the waste-basket. Even telephone solicitations—which are normally used only by small, local drives which could not in any event be pinched off by a Super Fund—can be handled courteously but firmly and briefly by the average, adult, self-possessed American. "All I do, unless it is some outfit I know I want to give to," says one professional man, "is simply say, 'Sorry, I never give by phone,' and hang up."

As for the Man in the Street, he is far from being annoyed by solicitation. "The little man," says one professional fund-raiser, "doesn't complain of annoyance; it's the executive," and a well-known labor leader, though he would welcome federation for his own convenience, says, "Multiple drives do not cause much annoyance to the Man in the Street."

Is It Intolerable, Even to be "Annoyed"?

Presently, we shall see some statistical evidence that people at large are not annoyed by multiple calls on their generosity. But let us concede that a minority of people are, and that to them the bright picture of freedom from bother is by far the most appealing argument in favor of a Super Fund.

Is this wise reasoning?

Charity is not a convenience. "Charity drives,"

says a prominent official of the New York Stock Exchange, "are a necessity, not an annoyance. It is a citizen's duty to give. There is no annoyance other than getting the work of the appeal done . . . People just can't slough off an appeal on the pretense that there are too many appeals." And a labor leader seconds him: "No drive is annoying if the cause is worthy."

An infinite number of things we need in this world, we get only at the expense of some annoyance. The schoolboy is annoyed by teachers and the youth by having to finish college. The husband is annoyed by wifely solicitude, and the wife by her husband's devotion to business. The world has been incessantly annoyed by thinkers with new ideas; Socrates, Confucius, Copernicus, Columbus, Newton, Darwin, Einstein. Indeed, it was in sheer arrogant exasperation that men once crucified a certain Carpenter of Nazareth—little thinking what an influence upon the world would be wrought by the "annoying" insistence of One who preached, "Blessed are the poor in spirit . . . they that mourn . . . the meek . . . the merciful."

Compassion, indeed, cannot exist without that troubling of spirit which comes from learning, somehow, that it is needed. "Annoyance" is a small price to pay for the spiritual uplift that comes from helping one's fellow men.

There is No Popular Demand for a Super Fund

Super Fund advocates are fond of representing that they are "armed with a mandate from the People." They like to give their proposal an air of spontaneity by claiming that it "started at the grass roots." It is one of those large claims so easy to make, especially when the maker has no figures to back it up. Until recently there were, in fact, no such figures. "No opinion poll has been taken," confessed the Gunn-Platt report in 1945, "[but] public health authorities . . . have claimed for over thirty years that the public is confused."

Well, in 1948 a cross-section sample of the public's attitude *was* taken—by an impartial and highly reputed market research organization, as described in the foreword of this book.

It was taken in two sections: one in the State of Michigan, where there had recently been a good deal of agitation for the Super Fund idea by Super Fund enthusiasts who had persuaded businessmen of considerable prominence to sponsor their cause, the United Health and Welfare Fund. This portion of the survey covered 1,006 men and women representing a statistically accurate cross-section of the people in Michigan. As a check to the findings of this survey, a similar survey was made among 3,992 people in other sections of the country, similarly selected to get an accurate cross-section of the country at large.

Most people interviewed *had never even heard of
any proposal for a federated drive:* 75.5% of people
in the country at large—*89.2% in Michigan itself,*
where the claim to a "mandate" had been made in so
many words. In that state, where "grass roots
origins" are most broadly claimed, not 11% of the
people had ever heard the Super Fund idea mentioned.

Wherever a person interviewed said he had never
heard of the Super Fund idea, or when he said he
could not remember, the investigator said:

> "The plan means that there will be one
> drive a year to collect all health and wel-
> fare funds. There are many arguments both
> for and against such plans. I would like to
> read the arguments on both sides to you."

Thereupon the investigator read *and showed* the
card which is reproduced on the opposite page.

The investigators, in keeping with sound research
practice, had no idea which side of the question was
favored by the sponsors of their work. But the argu-
ments on the card were phrased with such care to
avoid prejudicing people *against* the Super Fund
that there is evidence that some interviewers did in
fact imply by expression or tone of voice that the
federated idea was preferable. Yet even so—*and
plausible as the case for federated fund-raising is at
first sight—more people were against it than for it.*

REASONS IN FAVOR OF THE GROUPED PLAN

1. Some of the smaller state and national agencies fighting serious health problems might receive greater support.

2. Each county and state would have a fair share of the national total budget to raise.

3. Unified plan would reduce the total campaigning expense.

4. Multiple campaigns are confusing and annoying to the public.

REASONS AGAINST THE GROUPED PLAN

1. A unified plan does <u>not</u> raise as much money as do independent drives. <u>No</u> voluntary agency has ever raised as much money as it actually needs for a total job.

2. No one <u>must</u> give to any organization; joint fund raising takes away the freedom of the individual to give to the particular charity he is most interested in supporting.

3. The higher expense of voluntary fund-raising is justified by public awareness of the problem, resulting from campaign publicity, such as the valuable knowledge that cancer is curable if detected early.

4. The public has supported the drives of independent health agencies by contributing more each year to them, thus indicating its approval of the method.

Specifically, after the card had been read and examined, all people—including those who had already heard of the idea—were asked, "Which type of fund raising do you prefer?"

	In Michigan	In the Country at Large
Favor independent fund-raising	55.5%	52.1%
Favor group (federated) fund-raising	41.2%	42.8%
Don't know, or no opinion	3.3%	5.1%

We shall have occasion later to note some of the other opinions of people about various types of fund-raising, as shown by this survey. For the moment, the points to remember are two:

—Far from *demanding* a Super Fund, *most people have never even heard of the idea.*

—Plausible as the Super Fund idea seems, and vigorously as it has been pushed, *the majority of people are against it.*

Voluntary Workers are not Exhausted

A more serious argument against a multiplicity of drives is the one put forward by some thoughtful advocates of the Super Fund idea who are genuinely concerned with the cause of giving.

> "Multiple campaigns," they say, "are a drain on manpower—on leaders and volunteer workers. There simply are not enough willing workers to go around."

If this were true, it would be serious. But it is not true. The same leaders and workers are asked, and asked repeatedly—but only because fund-raisers take the easiest way and ask those who have already served.

Only about one-quarter of all people have ever been voluntary workers on fund-raising. Of those who have not, some 30% say they would be willing to serve (actually, 38.6% in Michigan). These were among the figures turned up in the nation-wide survey above referred to. It is perfectly evident that there is a great, untouched reservoir of American citizens who are ready and willing to carry on the work of fund-raising for charity, health and welfare if they are permitted to do so.

Funds Themselves do not Suffer from Multiplicity

Another favorite assertion of the Super Fund advocates is even more strikingly disproved by actual facts. They say:

> "Worthy causes suffer because . . . there is only so much money to be obtained . . . a necessary limit to what the public can contribute . . . It is out of the question to expect the public . . . to support half a dozen or ten or fifteen special organizations . . . The annoyance of multiple drives causes all agencies to suffer."

This is, to put it bluntly, arrant nonsense. It is at variance with all experience in business and in fund raising itself. In actual fact, the multiplicity of drives actually increases the sum total of all giving, and every drive indirectly helps every other one for reasons amply known to every economist and businessman.

To say that the public will not support more than one organization of a kind shows a singularly fatuous blindness. Let the theorists look around in their own communities. Any city, according to its size, will support half a dozen—or half a hundred—or more— motion picture theaters. What about hotels, restaurants, department stores, banks, churches, educational institutions? Let them look around the nation. We support four major and competing broadcasting networks, a dozen large mail-order houses, 23 makes of motor cars (not including trucks), 24 makes of tires, 48 or more brands of coffee, 106 makes of paint, 184 makes of shoes, and upward of 200 insurance companies—and all in competition for the attention and the dollars of the same public which is alleged to be incapable of supporting more than one health and welfare organization.

In fact, health and welfare agencies do not suffer from one another's competition. As Dr. Armstrong says in the previously cited article in the *Journal* of the American Medical Association, "The public is not averse to multiple agencies . . . During the last few years when the public was supposed to be consciously overburdened and annoyed, agencies have developed more rapidly . . . than in any equal period. Never have separate movements met with such generous financial support . . . Public interest and sympathy increase rather than shrink."

Statistical proof of this is available in many published sources. For example, the Community Chests' own central organization, in a bulletin dated July 1948, gives the total funds raised over a 14-year period by 253 continuously reporting member Chests. The figure for 1948 is *more than double* that of 1935.

This is not surprising to those who know the facts of mass human response from experience instead of from theory.

47

Among these facts is a great and significant one which small minds have trouble grasping, and which pedants seem never to have heard of. But modern businessmen are well aware of it, and it has been proved over and over again:

Competition, with Publicity, Actually Helps all Competitors

Many a druggist has discovered that when his competitor, a block up the street, put in a window display of face cream or toothpaste, *his own sales of that commodity showed a sudden upward trend*, even though he did not display that article and even though his competitor displayed a brand competing with that which he carried. This is common experience, repeatedly proved by figures cited in the business press. National manufacturers have found the same thing: When Pepsi-Cola started an intensive sales and advertising drive, some years ago, Coca-Cola, the established brand, not only did not lose sales, *but actually gained*. When Spry, the Lever Brothers' vegetable shortening, made its debut with strongly competitive advertising, the sales of Procter & Gamble's Crisco did not suffer—*they grew*. From 1929 to 1945 the sales of *all* meat packers grew, despite intensive competition, including that of a new company which built a $100 million business for itself from a $10 million start. The world of business is full of such instances, amply documented with figures running into many millions of dollars, based on nation-wide experience and covering years in time.

Why is this? There are several reasons—and they all apply to fund-raising as inevitably as to the promotion of sales in business:

Each competitor helps build up public awareness of the kind of product they all make. If only one motor car manufacturer, for example, were to advertise new cars, a great many people would still be content to get along with their old ones. But when all makers advertise and show new cars, the public becomes so acutely new-car-conscious that automobile workers cannot keep up with the demand. If only one insurance company were to advertise and push sales, the total amount of life insurance in this country would fall off sharply. Because numbers of them advertise and all of them drive hard with active solicitations, Americans are the best-insured people in the world.

Similarly, if only one charity organization were to publicize need and drive for giving, the public would think less often, less acutely—and with far less result— about giving. The very number of agencies

actively promoting charity, health and welfare, serves to increase public consciousness
of need and public readiness to give.

*A variety of competitors, each making a different
and distinctive appeal to the best of his ability, in-
sures that everyone will be approached on some responsive point.* A great number of appeals combined
in *one* campaign would only diffuse and weaken that
campaign. But a number of campaigns, each empha-
sizing a different appeal, reach, among them, practically everybody in the country. People who are deaf
to one appeal will respond to another. And even people responsive to various appeals, react best to a
cumulative working upon their consciousness by a
number of appeals *separately stated.* Thus, some
years ago one tire company promoted safety against
blowouts, another safety against skids, another
economy of long mileage, another ease of riding, another beauty of the then-new white wall tires, and so
on . . . The result was not that any one company progressed at the expense of the others, but that all
progressed, because people began taking care to get
new tires when they needed them instead of driving
around on old, battered, worn and unsafe tires.

—So it is with fund-raising. One agency
makes people aware of disaster relief,
others of tuberculosis, cancer, infantile

paralysis and similar perils. Other agencies get people to think carefully about social service, or character building, or education, or care of the handicapped ... And others, still, talk to them about the needs of local causes, local institutions ... The sum of this effort is not merely all-inclusive in the sense that it reaches the man whose interest is chiefly in the blind, as well as the woman whose great concern is for animals. It is cumulative in that it makes the average citizen realize deeply how vast is the work that needs to be done, and how intensely it needs his support.

The real "competition" of any company is not the direct competition afforded by its immediate competitors, but the indirect competition of other kinds of product. The Metropolitan Life Insurance Company's most serious competition is not that of Prudential or Equitable or New York or Guardian or Aetna or any of the others; it is the competition of new refrigerators and school tuition and Keeping Up with the Joneses and a thousand other calls upon the average man's budget.

—So the real competition of the Community Chest or the Red Cross is not that

afforded by the Christmas Seals or the
March of Dimes or any other drive. It
is the competition of golf club expenses
and entertaining and new fur coats and
movies and television sets. The American
public spends more than three times as
much for liquor annually as the sum
of *all* giving—to health and welfare,
charity, churches, endowments and everything else combined.

-As a corollary to this, there is no such
thing as "*a fixed amount of dollars available for charity.*" And though there is a
working limit to the amount any one man
will give at any one time, there is no such
thing as "*a limit to the amount the
American people will give to charity.*"

*Competition introduces vigor, life, new ideas, new
concepts* into every field. In business this is recognized. A firm learns from its competitors; it is
spurred by their success to outdo them with new
ideas, new enterprise, new use of techniques. All modern practice in radio and publication advertising, in
selling, in retail distribution and display grow out of
the stimulus of competition. In fact, it would now be
recognized as a sign of mental incapacity in a businessman merely to deplore the success of a competitor's methods without considering how to excel them.
Yet when the pedants of fund-raising contemplate

the success of such devices as the March of Dimes or the recent "Walking Man" contest, they hold up their hands and exclaim, in the words of the Gunn-Platt report, "Does anyone want to see this type of public solicitation multiplied?"

—The answer to that one is that if organized fund-raising wants to see the total amount of the public's giving rise by leaps and bounds, it has only to encourage—not deplore—a widespread use among all agencies of ingenuity and resourcefulness in appealing to people along the lines of human nature. The success of these fund-raising measures was due to the adroit use of good sense: the March of Dimes simply harvested by systematic and successful means millions of small coins previously overlooked by everyone except the Salvation Army. The Heart Association simply enlisted radio —to the advantage of both a radio program and itself—in a new kind of painless drive, utterly free from even a trace of "annoying" solicitation. The success of these and other envied and criticized measures, such as the Christmas Seal drive of the Tuberculosis Association, is not due—as is sometimes alleged—to any naturally superior dramatic interest of their beneficiaries. A child's pitiable plight is not inherently more compelling than a man's or woman's own fear of cancer or disabling accident, or his sympathy with people as old as he will some day be himself. *Any* cause can be presented forcefully, and there are a thousand untried ways to do so. What fundraising needs is more use of business common sense and ingenuity, and less of pedantic stuffiness.

In fact, the very faults of independent fundraising most criticized by the Super Fund advocates are its strongest points in actual present operation and in potential for the future of all giving in America.

Continuity of Appeal

"Hardly a month goes by," say those who favor a single drive each year, "without some cause making its plea to the public."

And why not? We have seen that the public is neither confused nor unduly annoyed by this continuity of appeal. We have seen that a single appeal once a year is not enough, and that the ordinary man or woman would rather give $5 every month or so than $20 at one time.

And we have only to observe the policy of every successful national manufacturer and advertiser, of every successful retail enterprise, to appreciate the fact that success in raising money, whether by the sale of merchandise or by the solicitation of contributions, is furthered by a year-round spacing-out of appeals.

This spacing-out is achieved by voluntary co-operation of the various agencies, national, regional and local, in the allocation among themselves of times for drives. Super Fund advocates are fond of asking, "If voluntary agencies can get together on a spacing-out of their drives, why can't they get together on one unified drive?" It is like saying, "If a dozen people can arrange to take turns at a bathroom, they ought to get together and all take a bath at the same time."

Enthusiasm of Supporters

It is always dismaying to Utopians when they encounter among those whom they would regiment, an enthusiasm for forging ahead in their own way. It is this keenness of personal interest in a cause which gives vitality to every drive from local Chests to national independent campaigns. And the vitality of separate drives combines in a cumulative effect upon the resultfulness of all drives. The end-product of many separate enthusiasms is to create an awareness, a responsiveness on the part of the public, which could never be achieved by the integration—however precise—of the same number of workers motivated by a general appeal.

Educational Value of Independent Drives

One important function of any health or welfare organization—whether independent or federated—is public education in its particular field: the cultivation not merely of a willingness to give, but of a readiness to cooperate the year 'round in measures which reduce disease, lessen the probability of injury, facilitate the work of professionals, secure the cooperation of government and citizens in legislation and in social work . . . and the like.

A considerable part of this educational work is accomplished in the course of fund-raising—a far greater part than the layman may realize. For the health or welfare agency's drive is its publicity campaign for its objectives, comparable to that of the advertiser, and like the advertiser's campaign, reaching out more widely than any closely applied educational material. The sum-total of such campaigns has had a tremendous influence upon American life, as your dentist, for instance, will tell you. And even the advocates of the Super Fund agree that the educational influence of national voluntary agencies is accomplished in large measure through their drive material. For example, the Gunn-Platt report says of the National Tuberculosis Association's Christmas Seal Campaign that the drive "itself embraces a considerable degree of health education."

The "Disorderly Order" of the American Way

Even the undisciplined individuality of multiple agencies is a source of strength in the typical American way. Super Fund advocates are fond of hunting for points at which the work of one independent agency overlaps that of another, and of digging up supposed examples of duplication of effort.

If the wastefulness of "indiscipline" is as bad in actual operation as it is in Utopian logic, then all the rest of American life is wrong: We manufacture a score of motor cars, where three at most would do—according to the Utopians . . . We have three or four department stores at a single crossroads, where one would do for a whole city . . . We support 800 colleges and universities, where a hundred regional ones would suffice . . . And so on through the entire range of everything Americans make and distribute and maintain as parts of our high standard of living.

Is this "disorder" in the American way of doing things *actually* wasteful? On the contrary, it is a factor in a *total increase* of national strength that far outweighs the minor loss of "disorder," "duplication" and "indiscipline" characteristic of freedom of enterprise. The Nazis created a disciplined and regimented economy much admired by Utopians; there was hardly a waste motion in the whole Reich. But even in its heyday, before the bombs began to fall, it proved measurably inferior in man-for-man production power to that of the "disorderly" but enterprising United States, with ten thousand firms working out their own "know-how" and scrambling for a chance to take up a small section apiece of the burden of wartime production. Russia has been trying for a quarter of a century to create an economy based on regimentation to eliminate "duplication" and "waste of effort." Yet even allowing for the destruction of war, that economy has been totally unable to produce the requirements of a standard of living even closely approaching that of the democratic nations. Control is not the only thing you need for high efficiency. There is a numbing effect of regimentation that destroys more than it saves. For while it saves pennies in slide-rule efficiency, it loses thousands and millions in lost opportunities, discouraged inventiveness, rebuffed initiative, unexercised enterprise, aborted enthusiasm.

In its way, too, the strength of American health and welfare work is due in very large measure to the "undisciplined" but free and untrammeled exercise of American enterprise. Charity and fund raising are not "unbusiness-like"; they are very like American business itself: characterized by a "disorderly order" which is the strength of the whole American system.

The Super Fund Idea is Dangerous

The entire concept of the Super Fund, desirable as it may be for the tranquillity of the giver and plausible as it is when presented in Utopian terms, is actually fraught with immediate peril to health and welfare work in the United States, laden with implications and bureaucratic regimentation and potentially destructive of the entire basis of giving.

It Would Immediately Reduce the Amount of Giving to Charity, Health and Welfare Work in America

By substituting for a present year-round sequence of intensive drives a single campaign with blunted and diffused appeal, the Super Fund would sharply reduce the amount of American giving. Indeed, the only undisputed "merit" of a Super Fund is the fact that it would ask people less pressingly to support charity, health and welfare agencies.

It Masks a Totalitarian Intent to Regiment American Health and Welfare

Businessmen are sometimes persuaded to front for the Super Fund movement by a profession of innocent and limited intent: The movement "has no thought of directing or influencing the sound programs of . . . agencies or submerging identities." It "intends to continue to work with agencies nationally" and "does not propose to usurp any of the functions or prerogatives of their boards of directors." In fact, it "proposes to do just one thing—effect a federation of fund-raising activities of the member agencies," providing them "adequate support . . . details [of which] will be worked out on the basis of mutual conference across the conference table." Or so the enthusiasts say, some of them doubtlessly in innocent good faith.

But actually, the intent of many prime movers in the Super Fund movement is to control all the operation of all controllable agencies from the largest down to those too small to be pressured—by control of their budgets. By insisting on passing upon policies and practices of agencies before allowing them to participate in the Super Fund, and by cutting down on funds at discretion, the Super Fund authorities would "promote the extension, the consolidation, the moderation or the elimination of service wherever desirable." Numerous prominent protagonists of the Super Fund idea make no secret of their intent to control agencies—by a totalitarian process of "liquidation." Says the National Information Bureau, proposed arbiter of worthiness for the Super Fund, "Some agencies have served their purpose and should be liquidated. Some operate below minimum standards of program and leadership and probably should be starved out of existence." (*Giver's Guide to National Philanthropy*, 1948–49.) And elsewhere the same organization proposes to give "priority attention" not merely to new organizations seeking recognition and help, but to established agencies which incur the arbiters' disapproval for being either unsuccessful *or successful*—"Old line agencies which have drifted into relative incompetence while still holding public favor, or which have expanded suddenly to a dimension of support beyond their leadership capacity or need."

Indeed, even in local Chests with less extreme intentions, it proves difficult, with all the good will in the world, to avoid dictating to member agencies, for in any grouped activity, the holders of the purse-strings find themselves with far greater power than anybody anticipated. As one Chest executive says,

"Although the Chest does not [normally] administer an agency, it does sometimes, when the old dollar sign shows up. In other words, the Chest cannot help but direct in some degree the agency's policies when they have control over the budget."

"Approval" as a Tool for Control

Super Fund advocates profess that the Fund would not "force anybody to join"; the national independent agencies need not federate except of their own free will. Yet the very form of local set-up on which a Super Fund would be modeled is one which includes as a primary activity for the Chest, recommending or disapproving agencies which would appeal to the public, even on their own, for funds. (85% of the review boards already established do this.) Disapproval, or even the withholding of approval, when that is combined with intensive publicity of the Chest's attitude, is aimed either to force agencies into the Chest, or to starve them out of existence. "No agency can survive for very long after it has lost the good will of the public."

Totalitarianism in Charity

If and when all agencies are obliged to come under a central control, the first essential of totalitarianism is achieved. Thence—as all world experience shows—the process inevitably proceeds to ever-tighter control by an ever-stronger central body, permitting no opposition, and ruling by decree.

"Two kinds of people," says Dr. Armstrong, previously quoted, "want . . . consolidation and . . . are willing to sacrifice freedom to regimentation with the object of economy, efficiency and more complete control: . . . organizers who are constitutionally inclined to favor other efforts at socialization . . . and business executives who . . . like the local Community Chest idea because it means fewer requests . . . and [because] actually in most instances they and their businesses will have to give less." The parallel to Germany is exact. There, too, totalitarianism came to power because businessmen did not stop to think-through the effect of their encouragement of what looked like "efficiency."

But not all businessmen are too hasty. Many of them say, like an executive of one of America's very largest corporations, "If one group were created to collect for and administer to all charities, it would become a Frankenstein which government and other officials would attempt to control, and which would lead into totalitarianism. Grouped activity is un-American, leading to centralization and 'impersonalization' which definitely have no place in charity work."

The Super Fund Would Go Beyond the Law

We have existing national laws which insure honest use of the mails. We have state laws and municipal regulations which safeguard the citizen from fraudulent individuals or organizations—and even, in many localities, from annoyance by other-than-registered solicitations. Few of us would go as far as the zealous clergyman advocate of Super Funds who favors "a government bureau, as strong as possible, and supported by taxation, to supervise and audit high-cost collections, insure good allocation of funds." In the opinion of many straight-thinking citizens, existing legal measures should be sufficient: "If an applicant meets the established [legal] tests," says a prominent labor leader, "granting of a license should be made mandatory." The public should be able to exercise a more reasonable, adult degree of judgment in matters of *relative* worth than any authoritarian body of officials could safely make for it.

And that holds true even more when the censoring body is not a governmental but a self-appointed group. Kluxism has no more place in charity and welfare work than it does in the social and economic relationships of a community. Even the best of people, with what seem to them like the purest of motives, have no license to regulate as vigilantes the affairs of their fellow citizens.

Group Coordination is One Thing;
Neighbor-Policing is Another

It is all very well for local charity, health and welfare agencies, associated in a local Chest, to agree to such measures of purely voluntary coordination as they may deem best within their own ranks and in their own territories. At the regional and state level, too, there are associations for the voluntary coordination of effort. And at the national level the national independent agencies—both within and without the National Health Council—coordinate their work with one another on a freely consultative basis.

But some local-level people are seeking through organization of a Super Chest to police and regulate not only all organizations in their own areas, but the national organizations in their nation-wide field as well. And since the national independents *in toto* form a much larger group, with combined funds far exceeding those of all local Chests put together, it is not to be wondered that they prefer to be left to coordinate their own activities in their own way. So the universities might feel about a proposal in high-school circles to bring them under a high-school-created control.

In the national independent agencies' view, a rigid, totalitarian control by even the best of Super Chests would be bad enough, for the many reasons this book sets forth. But that arbitrary control would be far worse when exercised—as proposed—by a Super Chest dominated by and taking its character, its pattern of operations and much of its personnel from local Chests.

It is not merely that there is inherent danger whenever a minority polices a majority. There is a very pointed threat to national agencies discernible in the existing policies of local Chest officials.

Regional Super Chests Show Bias Against National Agencies

It is common experience—and so reported by Chest executives themselves—that local Chests at best have some difficulty in viewing the needs and the contributions of national organizations in proper perspective. It is the exception that a national organization which tries federating with a local Chest gets an allotment for local purposes anywhere near its previous local budget or its contribution in current fund-raising to the total of the Chest. At worst, local Chest executives are actively opposed to national organizations—and for the most capricious of reasons: some because the nationals will not federate locally, others because certain nationals are "continually besieging" them to be allowed to federate locally. Others, again, suddenly decide that character-building organizations, such as the Y.M.C.A., should be thrown out of a local federated fund on the ground that character-building does not have sufficient appeal to fund-contributors, while still others engage in lengthy tirades against some of the national health agencies "because their causes have too great an inherent, dramatic interest."

A Super Chest dominated in large part by professionals with so partisan a bias against national independent agencies can hardly expect to "work with agencies nationally . . . providing them adequate support." It is not to be wondered that the nationals are gravely concerned at this aspect of the Super Fund project.

A Strait-Jacket upon Brotherly Cooperation

Nation-wide agencies are not the only ones upon which Super Chest authoritarianism would impose arbitrary and capricious restrictions. If the example already set by various appeals review boards is any indication, a Super Chest would seek to cut off interdenominational giving or indeed the support of any organization of special character by those who are not its immediate members. A Catholic organization may not solicit building funds from Protestants, nor a Protestant organization invite the support of Catholics or Jews for a city council of churches. The

Veterans of Foreign Wars are estopped from asking Legionnaires for comradely cooperation. A university may not seek endowments from others than its own graduates . . . It is not that the authorities are opposed to any one group; they are simply opposed to any fund-raising that does not fit certain arbitrary rules.

A Professional Bureaucracy in Charity

If one may judge from the character of incipient Super Chests—already being projected in some regions—a national Super Chest would be controlled largely by professionals drawn from the field of local Community Chest work. Review boards are typically financed in large part out of Community Chest funds and staffed with professionals either loaned by the Chests or "fortunately available" as former employees of Chests. As one prominent man remarks, out of some experience as a volunteer leader in fund-raising, "Grouped activities are [apt to be] operated by a hierarchy making a career of charity . . . [Their] allocation of funds is accomplished by internal politics . . . a group tends to become a bureaucracy."

A Super Chest Would Mean Super Pressure on the Giver

The local Community Chest—which is a small scale pattern in some respects for the proposed national Super Chest—exhibits one feature which nobody except fanatical extremists likes:

Because its appeal is so broad, generalized and diffused, the average Chest has to raise its budget by techniques which often include sheer pressure. This is admitted—regretfully enough—by Chest workers themselves, some of whom bemoan the necessity of "thumbscrew charity."

There is an interesting statistical reflection of this situation in the findings of the nationwide independent research quoted earlier in this book:

People were asked, "Why did you support such-and-such a charity?" Among the reasons cited, most, of course, were such as any man or woman would like to feel in giving—reasons that make giving a pleasure: belief in the cause, either on general impression or for specific reasons; a sense of civic duty and of unity with others in giving; lively interest as a member or participant; cheerful reaction to the type of drive . . . and the like.

But three groups of reasons for giving were different. In progressive degree, these three groups included more or less what people think of—perhaps not always justly, but nonetheless humanly—as "annoyance."

One group of reasons included, "worker called at home; collection at theater; booths; street solicitation." Not all of us would agree that these are "annoying," or even that if annoying they are undesirable. Yet because the Super Fund people represent them as instances of "pressure," we may concede that sometimes personal solicitations may be so called.

A second group of reasons included, "contributed at work; through employer; taken out of pay; mandatory at place of business." Here we have a broad class of reasons including at one end many cheerfully public-spirited cooperative moves, but at the other many undoubtedly pervaded by a spirit of compulsion (real or fancied) engendering a spirit of bitterness. All alike, however, come under the head of "annoyance" to the man or woman who would rather not be asked to give.

Lastly is sheer compulsion: "Don't particularly approve of or like their methods, but felt forced to give."

Now, it would be unjust to say that all people giving for any one of these three types of reason were under "pressure" in giving. Yet we can get at least a reflection of the comparative amount of pressure used by the principal fund-raising drives if we tabulate these reasons for giving as related to the various agencies' drives. Notice that the Community Chests got more of their money for reasons that included "pressure" than any other agency:

Per cent of people who gave because:

	Red Cross	Inf. Paralysis	Tuberculosis	Cancer	Sal. Army	Cripld. Child.	Boys Town	Comm. Chest
Worker called at home; collected at theater; booths; street solicitation...	19.4	13.7	9.7	12.8	17.9	8.1	15.9	15.5
Contributed at work; through employer; taken out of pay; mandatory at place of business	9.3	3.6	2.5	3.3	*	*	—	13.9
Don't particularly approve of or like their methods, but felt forced to give	2.2	*	*	—	—	*	—	2.7
Total response to "pressure".........	30.9	17.3+	12.2+	16.1	17.9+	8.1+	15.9	32.1

* less than 1%

ON A NATIONAL SCALE

Per cent of people who gave because:

	Red Cross	Inf. Paralysis	Tuberculosis	Cancer	Sal. Army	Cripld. Child.	Boys Town	Heart Fund	Comm. Chest
Worker called at home; collected at theater; booths; street solicitation...	16.0	14.5	6.5	13.2	14.9	3.2	7.1	9.8	15.5
Contributed at work; through employer; taken out of pay; mandatory at place of business	9.7	2.7	2.3	3.0	2.1	*	—	*	17.2
Don't particularly approve of or like their methods, but felt forced to give	2.2	.3	*	*	*	—	—	—	2.2
Total response to "pressure".........	27.8 [1]	17.5	8.8+	16.2+	17.0+	3.2+	7.1	9.8+	34.9

* Less than 1%. [1] Total is less than sum of the 3 individual reasons (27.9%) because 4 persons gave more than one reason for their answers.

Note that in both the above tabulations, Community Chest methods that included "pressure" are twice as high as those of most independent agencies, and that both in the State of Michigan and nationally, *Chests exercise most pressure at the place of employment.*

Other organizations do collect in offices and factories, but in practically no case do these agencies collect against a local or shop quota, with pressure put behind the drive by employers, department heads, supervisors, foremen and straw bosses. In such a drive—standard practice in Community Chest work wherever an employer's cooperation can be induced—the employee often feels *compelled* to give. And in very many cases that compulsion is bound up with a "check-off" system of deduction from the worker's pay envelope. That this practice is repugnant to employees need not be demonstrated to anyone who knows human nature. Employers do not like it, either, though they often cooperate from a feeling of civic obligation. It complicates their bookkeeping; it operates to impair good employee relations. But many people may be surprised to learn that representative union leaders, too, dislike the use of the "check-off" for employee contribution to fund-raising. The overwhelming majority of union leaders interviewed in the course of the survey are opposed to it. Their reason is that the "check-off," a device they favor in itself, is abused when the employee is "shamed" and "forced" into giving. A typical labor leader "would favor the check-off system only if strictly voluntary and revocable at any time. The employer should in no way . . . influence the decision of the employee." Another does not believe in the check-off for giving "unless on the basis of voluntary instructions by the employee without solicitation or attempt by the employer to shame the employee into participation"—and two others put it in almost the same words. An A.F. of L. leader and one from one of the Railway Brotherhoods state that their own unions "frown upon" deductions for these purposes and have discontinued consenting to them . . .

Experience of workers, employers and labor leaders alike combines to indicate that the check-off amounts to compulsion exercised upon the supposed "giver."

This is not *giving*. When charity is forced, more harm is done than the mere extortion of money from people who can often ill afford it. Thumb-screw fund-raising turns the spirit of generosity into bitterness, poisons the very wells of charity.

What America Needs Is More Giving

The trouble with American fund-raising is not that it needs control and regimentation—and certainly not that it reminds people too frequently of their opportunity to give—but rather that it needs still more to promote giving in the fullest sense of the word.

On a mere quantitative basis we do not give freely. The United States Treasury Department, in a release dated July 9, 1948, puts all America's claimed giving at only $1.5 billions—85/100 of 1% of national income. (The rosiest Utopian estimates do not claim we give over 1½%.) For most of us, giving is a matter of paring off as small a fraction of our money as will appease our consciences. We would be glad, indeed, if those consciences might be troubled less often—and the Super Chest idea is designed to gratify that wish. Yet many citizens—some of them in the most modest circumstances—give a biblical "tithe"—10% of their incomes. Without even approaching that measure of self-denial, without hardship and without strain, we Americans can give vastly more than we do—can begin to equip charity, health and welfare organizations with the funds to make this country really the land of freedom from want, fear and anxiety:

"Give all thou canst," said Wordsworth,
". . . high Heaven rejects the lore
"Of nicely calculated less or more."

But more than dollars, we need the warmth of heart which the very act of giving generates. We need an ever-present awareness that among our fellow men there are those who are weak when we are

74

strong, sick when we are abounding in health, needy when we are warm and fed, troubled in spirit when we are tempted to be complacent . . . We need to feel a sense of compassion, not once a year, or now-and-then by accident, but as a part of our daily attitude toward life. We need to think of giving not as a burden, but as an opportunity.